Address Book

Lesbian PULP

Susan Stryker

D1736181

CHRONICLE BOOKS

A portion of the proceeds from the sale of this book will benefit The Gay and Lesbian Historical Society.

Note on Permissions

Book cover art from *World Without Men* by Charles Eric Maine is reproduced by arrangement with the Berkeley Publishing Group, a member of Penguin Putnam Inc. All rights reserved.

Fees to reproduce images have been paid to the archival institutions housing the book covers included in this volume. Every effort has been made to locate the holders of copyrights of all the works reproduced, and to fairly compensate the owners for their use. No attempt has been made to infringe on any copyright.

ISBN 0-8118-2183-8

Manufactured in China

Typeset in Univers Ultra Condensed, Hoefler Text, and Trade Gothic

Design by Gayle Steinbeigle

Distributed in Canada by
Raincoast Books
9050 Shaughnessy Street
Vancouver, B.C. V6P 6E5

10 9 8 7 6 5 4 3 2

Chronicle Books LLC
85 Second Street
San Francisco, CA 94105
www.chroniclebooks.com

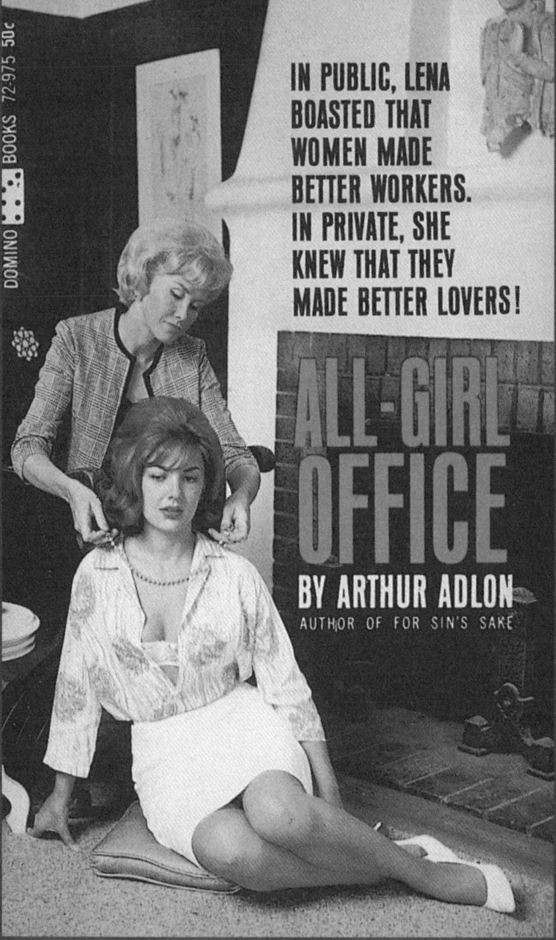
DOMINO BOOKS 72-975 50¢
IN PUBLIC, LENA BOASTED THAT WOMEN MADE BETTER WORKERS. IN PRIVATE, SHE KNEW THAT THEY MADE BETTER LOVERS!
ALL-GIRL OFFICE
BY ARTHUR ADLON
AUTHOR OF FOR SIN'S SAKE

A

Arthur Adlon, *All-Girl Office*
(New York: Lancer Books, 1965)

Lena Smith is a she-wolf. Women are
her prey, and she has created the
perfect hunting grounds—her own
consulting firm where the vivacious
female employees are "under her"
in more ways than one. Lena can't
figure out why a new hire, the
strangely assertive Geraldine
Powers, makes her heart beat
faster. Then she discovers "Gerry"
is a preoperative transsexual! If
Lena can restore Gerry to manhood,
she might make a normal marriage
for herself yet.

Name/Address

Phone/Fax/E-mail

Name/Address   *Phone/Fax/E-mail*

Name/Address

Phone/Fax/E-mail

Name/Address

Phone/Fax/E-mail

Their Love Was Right! But Their Sex Was Wrong

69 BARROW STREET

By SHELDON LORD

(an original novel)

K 35¢

✳
MIDWOOD

A Startlingly Frank Novel Of Love
In The Shadow World Of The Third Sex

B

Sheldon Lord, *69 Barrow Street*
(New York: Tower Publications, 1959)

B

Former art school chums Susan and
Sharon meet by chance on the side-
walk in Greenwich Village. Susan
has just moved to the city and
needs a place to stay. Sharon is
on the prowl for a new girl. Susan
isn't sure what shocks her more—
that her old friend has turned into
a shameless lesbian, or that Susan
herself returns Sharon's deep kiss-
es with an unexpected passion!

Name/Address   *Phone/Fax/E-mail*

Name/Address   **Phone/Fax/E-mail**

Name/Address   *Phone/Fax/E-mail*

Name/Address   **Phone/Fax/E-mail**

CINDY BABY

BY TONY TRELOS

BRANDON
75¢

SHE WAS A ROCK-AND-ROLL
LESBIAN WITH AN ANGEL'S
FACE AND A DEVIL'S BODY!

Tony Trelos, *Cindy Baby*
(North Hollywood: Brandon House, 1964)

Cindy is a hot-blooded young hipster
determined to sleep her way to
the top of the music business. She's
a nymphet willing to exchange her
body's pleasures for a shot at a
number one single. Cindy sets out
to seduce every powerful man in the
recording industry, but when that
rock-'n'-roll rhythm fills her soul,
she quickly discovers that only
women can satisfy the longings that
the beat stirs in her flesh!

Name/Address   **Phone/Fax/E-mail**

Name/Address   **Phone/Fax/E-mail**

Name/Address   **Phone/Fax/E-mail**

Name/Address   *Phone/Fax/E-mail*

_____   _____

_____   _____

_____   _____

_____   _____

_____   _____

_____   _____

_____   _____

_____   _____

_____   _____

_____   _____

_____   _____

_____   _____

_____   _____

_____   _____

_____   _____

_____   _____

_____   _____

_____   _____

_____   _____

_____   _____

_____   _____

Name/Address   **Phone/Fax/E-mail**

Name/Address   *Phone/Fax/E-mail*

DOMINO ▦ BOOKS 72-913 50¢

□□□□□□□ Their flaming desire
could only be satisfied by breaking
every rule and ignoring every taboo

duet in □□□□□
darkness

by Rea Michaels

author of □ □,□
Tw□ □ay Street

D

Rea Michaels, *Duet in Darkness*
(New York: Lancer Books, 1965)

In one of the rare lesbian pulp
novels to feature a woman of color,
fate has handed Laurie Russell a
spectacular body—and few other
advantages. Her no-good husband
can't satisfy her in or out of bed,
so Laurie looks elsewhere for love
and fulfillment. She finds it among
strange women whom society labels
"perverse." If only she had known
her escape from normality would lead
straight to a monstrous trap!

D

Name/Address   **Phone/Fax/E-mail**

Name/Address   **Phone/Fax/E-mail**

_____   _____

_____   _____

_____   _____

_____   _____

_____   _____

_____   _____

_____   _____

_____   _____

_____   _____

_____   _____

_____   _____

_____   _____

_____   _____

_____   _____

_____   _____

_____   _____

_____   _____

_____   _____

_____   _____

_____   _____

_____   _____

_____   _____

Name/Address   **Phone/Fax/E-mail**

Name/Address   **Phone/Fax/E-mail**

DWOOD

32-550

WINNER OF THE 1965 MIDWOOD AWARD
FOR LITERARY EXCELLENCE

ENOUGH OF SORROW

"A remarkably candid treatment of a
particularly controversial theme..."

JILL EMERSON

FIRST PRINTING ANYWHERE

E

Jill Emerson, *Enough of Sorrow*
(New York: Tower Publications, 1965)

The shocking story of a beautiful
young woman elevated from the depths
of despair and self-destruction by
the strange friendship of another
female. Together, Karen and Rae
boldly rip away the veil of mystery
that obscures the emotional and
physical aspects of lesbianism—
surely one of the most provocative
and misunderstood phenomena in
society today.

E

Name/Address   **Phone/Fax/E-mail**

Name/Address   **Phone/Fax/E-mail**

Name/Address   **Phone/Fax/E-mail**

Name/Address   **Phone/Fax/E-mail**

First person
3rd sex

The world of the les...the furtive
cult of strange loves and fierce passions.
by Sloane Britain

Sloane Britain, *First Person, 3rd Sex*
(Chicago: Newsstand Library, 1959)

The most predatory of all the sexes,
the lesbian competes for her mate
against men, against women, and
against social convention. Karen,
a sumptuous young schoolteacher,
charts her own course towards
happiness through a dangerous
no-man's-land of illicit love in
this shocking account of sensuous,
sapphic passion. Who knows which
beautiful women in our midst
secretly may be lesbians? Can any
unsuspecting young girl remain safe
from their unwholesome advances?

F

Name/Address   *Phone/Fax/E-mail*

Name/Address   **Phone/Fax/E-mail**

Name/Address　　　　　　　　　**Phone/Fax/E-mail**

Name/Address
Phone/Fax/E-mail

GAY GIRL

747-8   75¢

BY EDNA BRITT

THE DARK WORLD OF LESBIAN
LOVE HELD HER CAPTIVE!
COULD SHE EVER BE NORMAL
AGAIN?

G

Edna Britt, *Gay Girl*
(Las Vegas: Neva Pocketbooks, 1965)

Marilyn tries to deny her perverted
passions, but no stud ever seems
capable of doing for her all those
little things that come so naturally
to her lesbian lover. However
expert and attentive her male companion, however much she tries to
suppress the urge, she just can't
help but cry out the name "Nan" at
the height of her ecstasy. Can it
be true that Marilyn is destined
to find happiness only in the arms
of another woman?

G

Name/Address

Phone/Fax/E-mail

Name/Address   **Phone/Fax/E-mail**

Name/Address　　　　　　　*Phone/Fax/E-mail*

Name/Address   **Phone/Fax/E-mail**

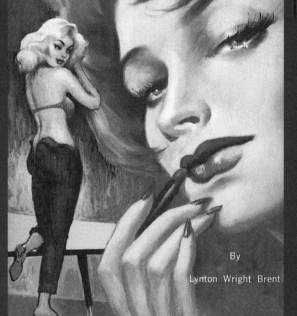

Lavender Love RUMBLE

95¢
FB
1013

By

Lynton Wright Brent

Lynton Wright Brent, *Lavender Love Rumble*
(Hollywood: Brentwood Publications, 1965)

Leslie Dane learns that nothing in
this world is really free—especially
"free love." Leslie is torn between
her mad affair with a famous lesbian
strip-tease artist and an equally
passionate fling with a rugged
Marine sergeant who has ravaged her
body and fanned the embers of her
soul. She realizes too late that
there is a price to pay for her
inability to choose between the two
sides of her desire—endless days
and sleepless nights tormented by
her own conscience.

Name/Address **Phone/Fax/E-mail**

Name/Address

Phone/Fax/E-mail

Name/Address

Phone/Fax/E-mail

Name/Address   *Phone/Fax/E-mail*

Daughter
of
Joy

35¢

NSL

By
James Harvey

She ruled her lesbian jungle with a bull whip—
and the passions that thrilled at its bloody snap!

James Harvey, *Daughter of Joy*
(Chicago: Newsstand Library, 1960)

Wealthy Stephanie Olson is determined to turn her private island
into a new Lesbos. Her statuesque
figure will rule supreme over the
lovely young converts whom she
plans to guide into the strange
by-ways of forbidden love. Stephanie
is smitten with a recent arrival—
the beautiful, dark-eyed Marie.
She is determined to keep Marie
away from Stephan, the arrogant
man foolish enough to raid her
all-woman world and claim the
island as his own!

Name/Address

Phone/Fax/E-mail

Name/Address   **Phone/Fax/E-mail**

Name/Address   **Phone/Fax/E-mail**

Name/Address   **Phone/Fax/E-mail**

HER REJECTED LOVE HURT WORSE THAN THE—

KNIVES OF DESIRE

By MORGAN IVES

AN EVENING READER

Morgan Ives, *Knives of Desire*
(San Diego: Corinth Publications, 1966)

When Fran joins the circus she is
willing to take any job at all
merely for the sake of survival.
In need of a protector in this
unfamiliar world, she thinks she
can trust Eva, a knife thrower with
an unusual taste for women. After
agreeing to become Eva's human
target, Fran realizes that perhaps
she should have learned a little
more about her volatile new friend—
and the bloody rages to which she
is prone!

Name/Address   **Phone/Fax/E-mail**

Name/Address **Phone/Fax/E-mail**

Name/Address   *Phone/Fax/E-mail*

Name/Address   *Phone/Fax/E-mail*

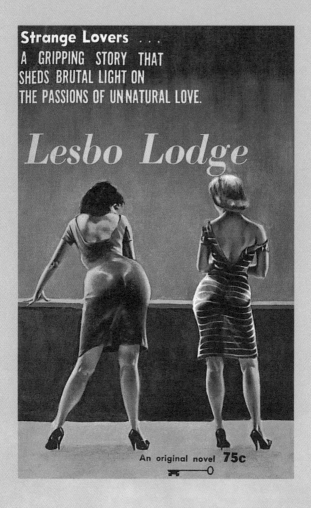

Strange Lovers . . .
A GRIPPING STORY THAT
SHEDS BRUTAL LIGHT ON
THE PASSIONS OF UNNATURAL LOVE.

Lesbo Lodge

An original novel **75c**

Harry Barstead, *Lesbo Lodge*
(North Hollywood: Private Edition Books, 1963)

It's dark. They're alone. She
finds herself beckoning, urging,
pleading with the other woman to
calm the angry fires of unquenched
lust ablaze within her own tormented
soul. Such scenes repeat themselves
nightly at Love Camp, the secluded
summer resort that caters to a
shadowy, sinister population of
female deviates.

L

Name/Address   **Phone/Fax/E-mail**

Name/Address

Phone/Fax/E-mail

Name/Address   *Phone/Fax/E-mail*

Name/Address   **Phone/Fax/E-mail**

_____   _____

_____   _____

_____   _____

_____   _____

_____   _____

_____   _____

_____   _____

_____   _____

_____   _____

_____   _____

_____   _____

_____   _____

_____   _____

_____   _____

_____   _____

_____   _____

_____   _____

_____   _____

_____   _____

_____   _____

_____   _____

_____   _____

_____   _____

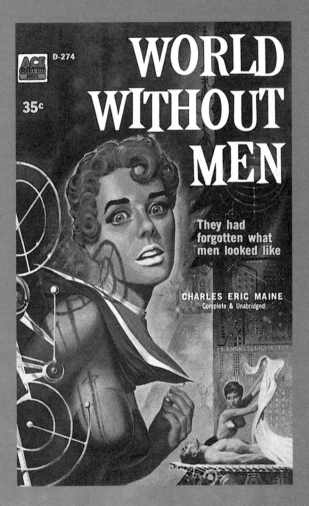

WORLD WITHOUT MEN

They had
forgotten what
men looked like

CHARLES ERIC MAINE
Complete & Unabridged

M

Charles Eric Maine, *World Without Men*
(New York: Ace Paperbacks, 1958)

Aubretia is a citizen of the world
5,000 years in the future—a world in
which women are the only sex and
babies are created in laboratories.
She can't quite put her finger on
the source of her vague unhappiness
until she is called in to view an
ancient human body—a man's body—
found buried beneath the Arctic ice.
Now that she knows what she's been
missing, nothing can stop Aubretia
from overthrowing her unnatural
matriarchal society.

M

Name/Address *Phone/Fax/E-mail*

Name/Address

Phone/Fax/E-mail

Name/Address　　　　　**Phone/Fax/E-mail**

Name/Address   Phone/Fax/E-mail

Name/Address

Phone/Fax/E-mail

Name/Address   **Phone/Fax/E-mail**

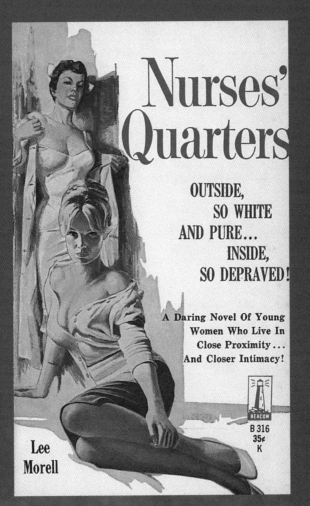

Nurses' Quarters

OUTSIDE, SO WHITE AND PURE... INSIDE, SO DEPRAVED!

A Daring Novel Of Young Women Who Live In Close Proximity... And Closer Intimacy!

B 316
35¢
K

Lee Morell

Lee Morell, *Nurses' Quarters*
(New York: Beacon Books, 1960)

Does lesbianism inevitably occur
when girls are herded together in
schools, at summer camps—or nurses'
quarters? Yes, the author of this
sensational portrait of women
without men dares to reveal. Young
Claire Hainsby's innocence has kept
her flesh so starved for love that
she easily falls victim to the
"experienced" Birdie Matthews. Now
Claire is reduced to battling the
sensual Nesta Johnson for Birdie's
cynical, self-serving attention.

N

Name/Address   **Phone/Fax/E-mail**

Name/Address   **Phone/Fax/E-mail**

Name/Address   **Phone/Fax/E-mail**

Name/Address   *Phone/Fax/E-mail*

ODD GIRL

Artemis Smith

B230
35¢ K

SHE FOUGHT — SHE STRUGGLED
— SHE EVEN MARRIED A MAN!
BUT IN THE END ANN
SURRENDERED TO TORTURED
WOMEN LIKE HERSELF . . . !

0

Artemis Smith, *Odd Girl*
(New York: Beacon Books, 1959)

Anne's feelings for Beth might have
passed for a young girl's crush, but
young girls shouldn't do what Anne
wants Beth to do to her—and Beth
seems only too willing to oblige!
Caught between the beastliness of
an emotionally damaged man who both
loves and despises her, and the
accepting softness of a woman who
offers both companionship and an
exhilarating sexual excitement,
Anne is poised on the brink of a
momentous decision—which lover,
which path in life, will she choose?

0

Name/Address   *Phone/Fax/E-mail*

Name/Address

Phone/Fax/E-mail

Name/Address   *Phone/Fax/E-mail*

Name/Address　　　　　　　**Phone/Fax/E-mail**

35c

story of a woman behind bars

PRISON GIRL

Wenzell Brown

Wenzell Brown, *Prison Girl*
(New York: Pyramid, 1958)

Linda is in protective custody. She
has committed no crime, yet hers
is the horrible life of any woman
behind bars. Every night she listens
to the soft sobbing of fellow
inmates ravished by sadistic guards,
and hears the husky whisper of a
would-be lady lover who says all
that Linda needs is the protection
of an older, experienced woman.
More than once Linda has seen the
flash of a switchblade rip a for-
merly lovely face to shreds. Maybe
the lady-lover is right.

Name/Address   *Phone/Fax/E-mail*

_____   _____

_____   _____

_____   _____

_____   _____

_____   _____

_____   _____

_____   _____

_____   _____

_____   _____

_____   _____

_____   _____

_____   _____

_____   _____

_____   _____

_____   _____

_____   _____

_____   _____

_____   _____

_____   _____

Name/Address   *Phone/Fax/E-mail*

Name/Address   **Phone/Fax/E-mail**

_____   _____

_____   _____

_____   _____

_____   _____

_____   _____

_____   _____

_____   _____

_____   _____

_____   _____

_____   _____

_____   _____

_____   _____

_____   _____

_____   _____

_____   _____

_____   _____

_____   _____

_____   _____

_____   _____

_____   _____

_____   _____

_____   _____

_____   _____

Name/Address   **Phone/Fax/E-mail**

She lived as a man, she fought as a man
she loved as a man

REBEL WOMAN

HARRY WHITTINGTON

An Avon Original

A
35¢
T-402
ICO

Harry Whittington, *Rebel Woman*
(New York: Avon, 1960)

In the Cuban revolution, women are
every bit as brutal as their male
comrades. American Jim Patterson
stumbles ashore only to be captured
by an armed brigade of girl commu-
nists. He's stunned to recognize
their leader, Captain Morales, as
his old sweetheart from home—and
to see the lustful way she now looks
at her lovely Lieutenant Dolores!
Patterson can only pray that one of
his captors is still woman enough
to be seduced by his manly charms.
Love is his only chance in a desperate bid for freedom.

Name/Address

Phone/Fax/E-mail

Name/Address   *Phone/Fax/E-mail*

_____   _____

_____   _____

_____   _____

_____   _____

_____   _____

_____   _____

_____   _____

_____   _____

_____   _____

_____   _____

_____   _____

_____   _____

_____   _____

_____   _____

_____   _____

_____   _____

_____   _____

_____   _____

_____   _____

_____   _____

_____   _____

_____   _____

Name/Address   **Phone/Fax/E-mail**

Name/Address   **Phone/Fax/E-mail**

THE
GO GIRLS

Will Laurence

They Rode
The
Nation's
Highways
On Their
Way To
Kicksville

First Publication Anywhere

s

Will Laurence, *The Go Girls*
(Derby, CT: Monarch Books, 1963)

Margo Thaxton and Dot Martin ride
with the Wildcats, a tough gang of
cycle-straddling vixens who grab
life by the throat and shake it
until they get what they want.
Margo's an out-and-out diesel dyke.
Dot's an ambisextrous wench who
reaches for her switchblade at the
slightest insult, real or imagined.
They're looking for kicks, kicks,
and more kicks—pity the poor man who
stands in their way!

s

Name/Address   **Phone/Fax/E-mail**

Name/Address   **Phone/Fax/E-mail**

Name/Address   **Phone/Fax/E-mail**

Name/Address   **Phone/Fax/E-mail**

Name/Address   *Phone/Fax/E-mail*

Name/Address   **Phone/Fax/E-mail**

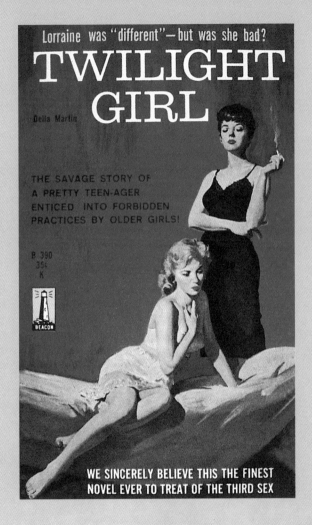

Lorraine was "different"—but was she bad?

TWILIGHT GIRL

Della Martin

THE SAVAGE STORY OF
A PRETTY TEEN-AGER
ENTICED INTO FORBIDDEN
PRACTICES BY OLDER GIRLS!

B 390
35¢
K

WE SINCERELY BELIEVE THIS THE FINEST
NOVEL EVER TO TREAT OF THE THIRD SEX

T
U

Della Martin, *Twilight Girl*
(New York: Beacon Books, 1961)

Lorraine Harris is an innocent
school girl seduced into perverse
practices by Violet, a pretty
blond carhop from the wrong side
of the tracks. Lorraine soon moves
on to Sassy, a rich and jaded
thrillseeker looking for a new
sort of sexual high. Next comes
Mavis, Lorraine's first "wife."
Lorraine doesn't mean to be bad—she
just can't control her passions.
Now it's too late to save herself
from the consequences of her own
confused desires.

T
U

Name/Address   *Phone/Fax/E-mail*

Name/Address   **Phone/Fax/E-mail**

_____   _____

_____   _____

_____   _____

_____   _____

_____   _____

_____   _____

_____   _____

_____   _____

_____   _____

_____   _____

_____   _____

_____   _____

_____   _____

_____   _____

_____   _____

_____   _____

_____   _____

_____   _____

_____   _____

_____   _____

_____   _____

_____   _____

Name/Address   *Phone/Fax/E-mail*

Name/Address   **Phone/Fax/E-mail**

_____   _____

_____   _____

_____   _____

_____   _____

_____   _____

_____   _____

_____   _____

_____   _____

_____   _____

_____   _____

_____   _____

_____   _____

_____   _____

_____   _____

_____   _____

_____   _____

_____   _____

_____   _____

_____   _____

_____   _____

_____   _____

_____   _____

_____   _____

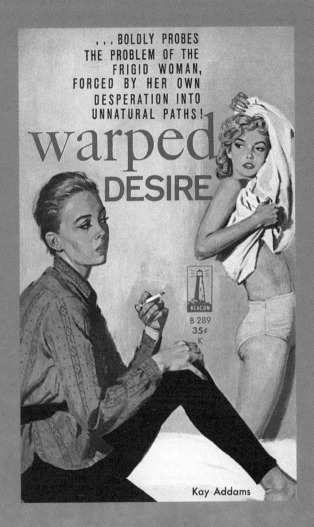

...BOLDLY PROBES
THE PROBLEM OF THE
FRIGID WOMAN,
FORCED BY HER OWN
DESPERATION INTO
UNNATURAL PATHS!

warped
DESIRE

B 289
35¢
K

Kay Addams

V
W

Kay Addams, *Warped Desire*
(New York: Beacon Books, 1960)

Frigid. That's Doris Fisher's
problem in a word. She tries to
awaken herself to normal passions,
surrendering to man after man, but
each new experience leaves her
feeling colder than the one before.
Not until a desperate Doris lets
lithe, lissome Laura Stevens
initiate her into the secret
mysteries of lesbianism does the
ice begin to melt!

V
W

Name/Address   **Phone/Fax/E-mail**

Name/Address   **Phone/Fax/E-mail**

Name/Address   **Phone/Fax/E-mail**

Name/Address

Phone/Fax/E-mail

LESBIAN TWINS

WILLI
PETERS

Vega Book 50¢

Obedient to Mom's insistence, Hilda
started upstairs to join Jane for a nap.
Jealousy stabbed at Bill's heart as
the ugly visions multiplied in his brain.

Willi Peters *Lesbian Twins*
(Fresno, CA: Vega Books, 1960)

Jane and Hilda's mother makes them do everything just the same. They dress alike and spend all their time together. So it's only natural that their first halting steps toward sensual pleasure should unnaturally arise from each other's fingertips. Each of the identical twin sisters knows the other's body as intimately as if it were her own. Now no man can ever satisfy them so well!

X
Y

Name/Address   **Phone/Fax/E-mail**

Name/Address   **Phone/Fax/E-mail**

Name/Address   **Phone/Fax/E-mail**

Name/Address   **Phone/Fax/E-mail**

B795X K

THE ODD KIND

Arthur Adlon

UNVEILS THE SLEEK AND EXPENSIVE WORLD OF THE LESBIANS WHO MODEL FASHIONS IN PUBLIC—AND PERFORM AGE-OLD RITUALS IN PRIVATE!

3rd BIG PRINTING

Z

Arthur Adlon, *The Odd Kind*
(New York: Softcover Library, 1962)

This story of love between women is set in the cosmopolitan dress salons of chic Manhattan, where the same old sins are recut to fit today's fashions. Once, luscious La Modena had been plain-jane Emily Jones. Now she's a high-priced super model who lavishes her attention on up-and-coming competition Pam Elliot—all the while keeping her well-coifed head looking over her shoulder for Pam's vicious, vindictive ex-girlfriend Haze!

Name/Address   **Phone/Fax/E-mail**

Name/Address   **Phone/Fax/E-mail**

Name/Address   **Phone/Fax/E-mail**

Name/Address   **Phone/Fax/E-mail**

Notes

Notes

Notes

Notes

Acknowledgements

Working on this project and its companion volume, *Gay Pulp*, has been a lark. Thanks to Craig Hetzer, Leigh Anna Mendenhall, and Gayle Steinbeigle of Chronicle Books for their support of this project; Pat Ackre, Tim Wilson, Susan Goldstein, Jim Van Buskirk, and the rest of the staff at the San Francisco Public Library for their help with the Barbara Grier/Donna McBride Collection; Willie Walker and Paula Jabloner of The Gay and Lesbian Historical Society of Northern California for help with the Patrick Butler Collection; Allyson Belcher for her photographic copy work; David Seubert for his informative Web page on gay pulp fiction; Allison Austin, Ed Polish, and the staff at Kayo Books in San Francisco for information provided on copyrights and permissions; Jordy Jones and Stafford of Service Station Design for consultation on electronic retouching; and to Kim Klausner and all the other people I pestered to look at selections from over a thousand pulp novel covers while I was trying to pick my favorites. Special thanks to my partner Kim Toevs, and our kids Wilson and Denali, just for having me around.

Like trashy
lesbian novels?

Many of the items featured in this address book, and more like them, were discovered in the archives of The Gay and Lesbian Historical Society of Northern California. The GLHS houses one of the nation's largest collections of historical material, documenting the lives of lesbians, gay men, transgendered people, and bisexuals. Besides spirited artwork like the pulp covers featured in this book, there is also a rich variety of documents, photographs, audiotapes, and artifacts that chronicle the emergence of vibrant and vital sexuality-based communities in the United States. The GLHS is a valuable resource not only for students and teachers of history at all educational levels, but also for graphic designers, multimedia artists, filmmakers, community organizers, policy makers, political activists, and anyone else who's curious about past and present sexual diversity issues.

Visit the GLHS website at www.glhs.org to learn more about its collections and how you can become a member and support its work. The offices and archives are located at 973 Market Street #400, San Francisco, California 94103. Phone (415) 777-5455.

Don't forget to buy the companion volume, the *Gay Pulp* address book!

Gay and Lesbian Historical
Society of Northern California/
Center for the History of Sexual Diversity
www.glhs.org